Take Two Tablets Daily

The 10 Commandments And 613 Laws

Angus Wootten

Take Two Tablets Daily
The 10 Commandments And 613 Laws

Special Thanks

Special thanks and appreciation to
Dr. David Cavallaro, and his wife Gloria
(Author, *My Beloved's Israel*),
whose support and encouragement
made this book possible.

"YHVH's
Covenant...is,
the Ten Commandments..."
(Deuteronomy 4:13).

CONTENTS

1

Under The Law?

Y*ou are trying to put me under the Law!*

This is often the cry from many Christians when it is suggested to them that the Laws and Commandments of YHVH are still valid.

If we suggest that the Laws and Commandments continue and have merit, does it mean we are looking to our keeping of them for our salvation?

No!

We gain acceptance by YHVH, through faith in Y'shua (Jesus), and not by observance of the Laws and Commandments. Salvation is by grace, which means we do absolutely **nothing** to merit or receive salvation. It is the free gift of YHVH.

It is only when we accept this gift, and experience the second birth into YHVH's family, that we can begin to do something about our own destiny. When we are born again, we are spiritual babies, and like physical babies, we begin to grow.

Our present physical being (mind and body) is the result of the care, diet and training we have given it. Our observance of the good health practices and physical laws will play an important part in determining whether we end up with the best mind and body possible. Remember, while the body always matures, it is a rare individual whose mind even begins to approach its full potential.

The same is true of our spiritual being. Our spirit is going to grow, and the extent of our spiritual maturity will be the result of the care, diet and training we give or allow it to have.

The practices, traditions, and regulations that guide us through life will determine what we do with our gift of salvation—and to what extent we realize our spiritual and physical potential.

The purpose of this book is to thoughtfully and rationally examine the precepts YHVH provided through Moses, for the express purpose of the physical and spiritual guidance of His people Israel.

What relevance, if any, do the laws have for us today? Can the principals contained in the Law of Moses improve the practices, traditions and regulations that we use in reaching for our maximum spiritual and physical potential?

This book is written with the hope that it will help answer these questions.

We start by examining the attitude the Author of the New Covenant had toward the Law (which was written by men under the inspiration of the Ruach ha Kodesh). At the same time we remember that this is His second book—for He also authored the Old Covenant.

"In the beginning was the Word, and the Word was

with YHVH, and the Word was Y'shua.. He was in the beginning with YHVH. All things came into being by Him, and apart from Him nothing came into being that has come into being" (John 1:1-3).

Take Two Tablets Daily

2

Y'shua's Attitude Toward The Law

The Apostle John, in his first epistle says, "The one who says he abides in Him ought himself to walk in the same manner as He walked" (1 John 2:6).

Even the Pharisees recognized that Y'shua was a "good man," which meant that He kept the Law (John 7:12). What they did not recognize were His messianic claims (Matthew 27:22; Luke 23:2). This attitude continues among Jews in our day. However, Jews, who have not accepted Y'shua as their Messiah do approve of the manner in which he walked.

Should we not also recognize that keeping YHVH's Law is a good for us?

Let us be real. If Y'shua returned today would we tell Him to: Get a haircut, quit your wine bibbing, keep away from sinners, realize that pork and shell fish are good for you, change your Sabbath to Sunday, liberalize your views on tithing, sex, family, what you can allow your eyes to see and your ears to hear, etc. etc.?

Y'shua, His disciples, and the Early Church recognized the authority of the Scriptures. From Y'shua's temptation to His crucifixion, the high moments in His walk were punctuated by citations from Scripture: "It stands written" (Matthew 4:4,7,10). "Not the smallest letter or stroke shall pass away from the Law" (Matthew 5:18). "Scripture cannot be broken" (John 10:35). These examples serve as persuasive witnesses to Y'shua's regard for His Father's Word.

What Y'shua condemned was **misuse** of the Law. Throughout His life, in all His teachings, Y'shua confirmed the validity of the Law. However, He always pointed out its proper use. Throughout His public ministry Y'shua denounced those who would interpret the Law mediatorialy (making the Law a mediator between man and YHVH). They were errantly setting the Law forth as a means whereby man could gain acceptance with YHVH.

Y'shua further opposed the externalization (outward appearance or behavior) of the Law; by which one would suppose that a man's relationship to YHVH is determined simply by an outward conformity to a set of laws, rules, or regulations.

Can we please Y'shua with an attitude towards the authority of Scripture that is any less than the example He set? Should we not have the heart attitude of the disciple whom Y'shua loved?

"My little children, I am writing these things to you that you may not sin. And if anyone sins, we have an

Advocate with the Father, Messiah Y'shua the righteous; and by this we know that we have come to know Him, if we keep His Commandments. The one who says, 'I have come to know Him,' and does not keep His commandments, is a liar, and the truth is not in him; but whoever keeps His word, in him the love of YHVH has truly been perfected. By this we know that we are in Him: The one who says he abides in Him ought himself to walk in the same manner as He walked" (The First Letter of John 2:1,3-6).

Take Two Tablets Daily

3

Our Need For Law And Order

The success of people living and working together is dependent on their mutual observance of agreed standards of conduct.

To this end families have their rules, companies their policies, social organizations their by-laws, and governments their regulations and laws.

Nowhere are standards of conduct more clear than in the area of religion. Every denomination, congregation, fellowship, etc., has its traditions, doctrines, theology, rules, and laws to govern individual and corporate conduct.

However, human history, and the condition of the world today, witness that mankind has not been able to develop a successful set of standards. The best attempts at developing workable standards of conduct have been in those countries and religions that have borrowed from and built upon a Christian/Judaic heritage. And, if America, with 1586 faiths representing the worlds major religions, each with a different set of standards and laws, is the best example of these attempts, then we are in trouble.

America: mammoth drug problems, soaring crime rates, five million homeless, and economic problems that include increasing unemployment and a three trillion dollar national debt. Yet, America's greatest problem is the battering the family has taken. Sexual freedom, including the acceptance of homosexuality as an alternate life style, has caused a collapse in sexual morality. This collapse has resulted in: A fifty percent divorce rate, millions of abortions annually, and an epidemic of sexually transmitted diseases. Surely, we have gotten lost on our way to Utopia.

Still, secular humanists and New-Agers believe man can create moral and decent societies—without YHVH. Then again, there are Christian humanists that believe they can *borrow* rules from both YHVH *and* man, and thus develop a set of religious standards that will do the job.

The problem today, and throughout history, is best described by the last verse of the Book of Judges: "In those days there was no king in Israel, everyone did what was right in his own eyes."

However, there will be a day when the Kingdom of YHVH will be established on earth. And, His kingdom will have a single, successful, set of standards. "YHVH will dwell among His people, and He shall wipe away every tear from their eyes, and there shall no longer be any death; there shall no longer be any mourning, or crying, or pain" (Revelation 21:3-4).

4

YHVH's Law Or Man's Law?

Sooner or later, the day will come when Y'shua's prayer, "Thy kingdom come on earth as it is in heaven," will be a reality! If we believe this, then we who have the Spirit of YHVH dwelling within us should be forerunners, in the spirit of Elijah, in establishing the Kingdom of YHVH here on earth.

One way we can do this is to allow YHVH to write His Law on our hearts. With His Law written on our hearts, we will be living in the Kingdom of YHVH, regardless of where the world is at in regard to the kingdom. For, while we are in this world, we are not of it. This is what the New Covenant is all about: Being of another world.

What law will YHVH begin to write on your heart as you progress towards spiritual maturity? What standards will YHVH use in determining your part in the world to come?

Paul, in the book of Romans, made it clear that there is no sin where there is no Law (Romans 5:13). Therefore, the only sins that we will be held accountable for by YHVH are violations of His Law.

Hosea, who was a prophet to the Northern Kingdom (Ephraim), stated that YHVH's people are destroyed for lack of, and rejection of, knowledge. Hosea said that this lack and rejection resulted from the people having forgotten the Law of YHVH their God (Hosea 4:6).

The question is not whether YHVH will hold us accountable for violating Laws and Commandments which we did not have the opportunity to know. Rather, the questions will be, did we refuse to receive the truth? Did we willfully choose to live in ignorance?

5

Paul And The Law

The Church's emphasis on the writings of Paul has resulted in Christianity giving more weight and authority to his epistles and letters than is given to the Old Covenant, or even the rest of the New Covenant.

Paul's writings make up approximately five percent of the Bible, and while they are Holy Scripture, neither Paul nor the Holy Spirit would have more weight and authority given to them than any other portion of Scripture. By neglecting certain parts of the Bible, we ignore Paul's declaration that, "All Scripture is YHVH-breathed and is useful for teaching, rebuking, correcting and training in righteousness" (2 Timothy 3:16, NIV).

Paul's Epistles, like any other part of Scripture, must be viewed in the light of the entire Bible. This means, when we are dealing with the Law, we must not focus in on only a few statements Paul made, while ignoring everything else the Bible says about YHVH's

Law. Instead, Paul's writings must be understood in a way that will make them compatible with what the other ninety five percent of the Bible says. In other words, rather than having Paul's five percent interpret the other ninety five percent, let the other ninety five percent of the Bible interpret the five percent that Paul wrote!

It is important to remember that Paul's letters were not meant to be theological treatises. Most of them represent his response to a particular situations in a specific city and a particular congregation. Therefore, we must have knowledge of the situation, or situations, Paul was addressing if we are to understand his writing in context.

Sometimes the problem can be understood from Paul's remarks, but often we are left with little or no knowledge of the situations Paul was dealing with.

Unfortunately, many people come to an understanding of Paul' writings that seems to contradict what the rest of the Bible teaches. This happens when people incorrectly reconstruct the historical background, or ignore it altogether.

We are not alone in encountering difficulty in attempting to come to a clearer understanding of what Paul taught. The Apostle Peter warns that Paul's writings are not easy to understand: "His letters contain some things that are hard to understand, which ignorant and unstable people distort, as they do the other Scriptures, to their own destruction" (2 Peter 3:16, NIV).

Those with little or no knowledge of the Old Covenant Scriptures are especially apt to misinterpret Paul's writings, and that to their own ruin. For it is not

Torah-observant Believers who distort Paul's epistles. Instead, it is the "lawless men" that Peter warns us about (2 Peter 3:17, NIV).

Paul's Positive Statements About The Law

Paul writes: "the law is holy, and the commandments are holy, righteous and good" (Romans 7:12, NIV). And, "In my inner being I delight in YHVH's law." And, "I myself in my mind am a slave to YHVH's law" (Romans 7:25, NIV).

Paul wrote to Timothy, "We know that the law is good if one uses it properly" (1 Timothy 1:8, NIV). To the Corinthians he wrote, "Keeping YHVH's commands is what counts" (1 Corinthians 7:19, NIV). Even when explaining the righteousness that comes by faith, he was careful to make it clear that the law is not to be abandoned: "Do we, then, nullify the law by this faith? Not at all! Rather, we uphold the law" (Romans 3:31 NIV).

Paul's "Negative" Statements About The Law

Paul, in his **supposed** negative statements about the Law, was not criticizing the Law itself, but man's misuse of the Law. Paul knew that the Law was meant to be a moral guide, even for people already justified by faith. But some people in Paul's day, were trying to be justified by keeping the Law. What Paul criticized was not law-keeping itself, but people making law-keeping the basis of one's justification before YHVH.

Between the Babylonian captivity and the time of Y'shua, Israel developed an erroneous understanding of the law's purpose. The Jews who returned from Babylon knew that their exile had been the result of breaking YHVH's laws; therefore, they put a new emphasis on keeping the Law.

Unfortunately, this new emphasis eventually caused people to erroneously view law-keeping as the key to their justification, rather than being justified by faith, as was our forefather Abraham. Paul's supposedly negative statements were simply his attempt to correct this erroneous use of the Law.

One writer puts it this way: "Paul, in his epistles, affirms the Law, yet he condemns the wrong emphasis men place upon it. It is in this sense that Paul is turning believers back to the original intent of the Law. For the Law is a rule for godly living for those who are already redeemed. Paul rejects the later shift towards making it a means of salvation.

Samuel Bacchiocchi , in his book, *Sabbath in the New Testament,* [A] says basically the same thing. He writes, "Paul rejects the Law as a *method of salvation* but upholds it as a *standard of Christian conduct.*"

Paul's Example

Actions speak louder than words. And Paul faithfully practiced the Law. But before he met Y'shua,

---

A Page 101. *Sabbath in the New Testament,* p 101, Samuel Bacchiocchi,. 1985. University Printers, Berrian Springs, MI he kept the Law in an effort to be *justified* by his actions. After meeting Y'shua, Paul came to understand that we are justified by faith. Armed with his new understanding the law came to be internalized, it was "written upon his heart." Thus, Paul now had a desire to observe YHVH's Laws and Commandments, because of the inward impulse of his new nature. His obedience was no longer a result of an external compulsion to justify himself before YHVH. Now he was free to obey "in the new way of the Spirit, and not in the old way of the written code" (Romans 7:6 NIV).

The key to living a godly life in Messiah is not to ignore the Law and to elevate Paul, as many have done. Nor is the solution to over-emphasize the Law and reject Paul, as many have done. Rather the solution is to do what Paul said to do: "Follow my example, as I follow the example of Y'shua" (1 Corinthians 11:1 NIV).

Early in His ministry, Y'shua spoke this warning to His followers: "Do not think that I have come to abolish the Law or the Prophets; I have not come to abolish them but to fulfill them. I tell you the truth, until heaven and earth disappear, not the smallest letter, not the least stroke of a pen, will by any means disappear from the Law until everything is accomplished. Anyone who breaks one of the least of these commandments and teaches others to do the same will be called least in the kingdom of heaven, but whoever practices and teaches these commands will be called great in the kingdom of heaven" (Matthew 5:17-19, NIV).

Sometimes it is easier for people outside

mainstream Christianity to see the blindness of Christians in this area. And, the Jewish Encyclopedia[B] does quote Y'shua's warning of Matthew 5:17, and then makes this bold statement: "The rejection of the Law by Christianity, therefore, was a departure from its Christ..."[C]

B Volume 5, p 52, Jewish Encyclopedia, 1903. Funk and Wagnalls, New York, NY.

C Much of the material in this chapter is based on *The Ghost of Marcion*, an article by Daniel Botkin, printed in First Fruits of Zion Magazine, April, 1994.

6

Principles Of The Protestant Reformation

The Protestant Reformation was built on the foundational truth that man stands as a free, autonomous person before his God; and that man's dependence for his eternal welfare is on God Almighty alone. Nothing can come between YHVH and man except an instrument (medium) through which YHVH works. However, this instrument cannot become an authority over man, even though YHVH's authority may be transmitted through that instrument.

Martin Luther, whom we must acknowledge as being a perpetrator of anti-Semitism, also is the man whom many consider to be the father of the Protestant Reformation, and Luther made some interesting points that expand on the above principles:

"A Christian is the most free lord of all, and subject to none; a Christian is the most dutiful servant of all, and subject to everyone. One thing, and one alone, is necessary for life, justification, and Christian liberty; and that is the most holy Word of God, the Gospel of Christ, as He says: 'I am the resurrection and the life; he that believeth in me shall not die eternally'" (John 11:25).

"It is not by working, but by believing that we glorify God and confess Him to be true. On this ground [basis] faith is the sole righteousness of a Christian, and the fulfilling of all the commandments. For to him who fulfils the first commandment: 'Thou shalt worship one God only,' not by works but by faith of heart, will find the task of filling all the others easy."

"True then are these two sayings: Good works do not make a good man, but a good man does good works. Bad works do not make a bad man, but a bad man does bad works. As Jesus says: 'A good tree cannot bring forth evil fruit, neither can a corrupt tree bring forth good fruit' (Matthew 7:18).

"It is not from works that we are set free by the faith of Jesus, but from the belief in works, that is, from foolishly presuming to seek justification by works. For works justify no man, but a man must be justified before he can do any good work."

"We cannot live in the world without ceremonies, traditions, laws and works; since the hot and inexperienced period of youth has need of being restrained and protected by such bonds; and since everyone is bound to keep under his own body by attention to these things; therefore, the minister of Jesus must be prudent and faithful in so ruling and teaching the people of Jesus in these matters that no root of bitterness may spring up among them, and so many be defiled, as Paul warned the Hebrews; that is, that they may not lose the faith, and begin to be defiled by a belief in works, as the means of justification. This is a thing which easily happens, and defiles very many, unless faith be constantly inoculated along with works. It is impossible to avoid this evil when faith is passed over in silence, and only the ordinances of men are taught."

"Hence, in the Christian life, ceremonies, traditions, laws, and works are to be no otherwise looked upon than builders and work-men look upon those preparations for building or working, which are not made with any view of being permanent or anything in them-selves, but only because without them there could be no building and no work. When the structure is completed, they are laid aside. Here you see that we do not condemn these preparations, but set the highest value on them; a belief in them we do condemn, because no one thinks that they constitute a real and permanent structure."

In other words, Martin Luther is saying, "You need a form when pouring cement, a scaffold when building a wall. However, once the cement has hardened, and the wall is up, we not longer need the form and scaffold.

Unfortunately, the church today is so busy building their forms and scaffolding (organizations that supposedly help *us* who are the true temple to grow up in Messiah), that they have forgotten all about pouring concrete (making strong Believers that can stand on their own), and building *them* up, that they might stand like a steadfast *wall* against the enemy.

7

What Attitude Should We Have Toward The Law?

Some might point out that we are not under the Law, but rather under grace, and faith. While this is true regarding our salvation, Paul and James make it clear that we establish the Law with our faith.

Further, we have shown that we cannot live and work together without standards and laws, so we ask: Does it make sense that because we have been saved by grace that we will now make the choice to live under standards and laws made by men—whether those men be secular humanists, Catholics, Baptist or Jews? Should we abide by the laws of mere men rather than the Standards and Laws handed down by the Holy One of Israel?

What is the basis of YHVH's Standards and Laws? Is it the Ten Commandments which He spoke to our forefathers at Mount Sinai, and later engraved with His own finger in stone? He outlined His standards, not only to Moses, but to all those through whom He spoke in His Word—Genesis to Revelation. These standards, as basically recorded in the books of Exodus, Numbers, Leviticus and Deuteronomy, were not given to punish Israel, but to give them the opportunity to be the happiest, healthiest and wealthiest people on earth.

There is no pat answer to these questions. Questions, which in essence deal, with the challenge of incorporating the will and desires of YHVH in our lives. Again YHVH has not revealed everything. Rather He has revealed, and continues to reveal, to each of us what He wants us to know. While the "Law" He has promised to write on our hearts may not be verbatim according to the instructions He gave to Moses—which Judaism has codified into The Six Hundred and Thirteen Laws—still it will surely contain the same principles. Because, both were written by the same Author. And, that Author is the same yesterday, today, and forever.

It is our task to know when it is YHVH, that is writing on our heart and when it is not Him, but another. In accomplishing this goal we have as a valid tester His Word—Genesis To Revelation—together with the witness of the Ruach ha Kodesh.

We are to be workmen who accurately handle the Word of truth. We know that all Scripture is inspired by YHVH, and is profitable for teaching, for reproof, for correction, for training in righteousness. Therefore, a good place to start in determining the standards and laws of the Holy One of Israel, is with the commandments and instructions given to Moses.

The Decalogue, or Ten Commandments, are familiar to all Christians and Jews; however, the 613 Laws, 365 of which are positive (to do) commands, and, 248 which are prohibitions (forbids), are not as well known—especially to Christians.

Due to the absence of Christian sources, we have relied on Judaic sources for the order and rendition of the 613 Laws. As you read through them, realize that Y'shua fulfilled the sacrificial Law. However, as you study the other Laws, and even those that deal with sacrificial matters, we ask you to look for the principle. As you unearth these principles you will have a better understanding of the Loving Instructions, that YHVH gave us for our well-being.

YHVH's Word is medicine. And, nothing is more symbolic of His Word than the two tablets on which He wrote His Ten Commandments.

Taken daily, these two tablets will give us life. If we follow the Author, we will have life more abundantly, in this world, and eternal life in the world to come.

As you study YHVH's Laws and Commandments, you will gain a deeper insight into the writings of the Apostles. Because their writings assumed the reader knew YHVH's Laws and Commandments. And, you will have a better understanding of the earthly ministry of Y'shua, since He kept the Laws and Commandments of His Father.

May only the Spirit of the Holy One of Israel be your Guide as you read His Commandments and the following 613 Laws.

8

The Decalogue: The Ten Commandments

He declared to you His covenant which He commanded you to perform, that is, the Ten Commandments; and He wrote them on two tablets of stone (Deuteronomy 4:13).

1.   I am the YHVH thy God, who brought thee out of the land of Egypt.

2.   Thou shalt have no other gods before Me. Thou shalt not make unto thee a graven image, nor any manner of likeness, of any thing that is in heaven above, or that is in the earth beneath, or that is in the water under the earth; thou shalt not bow down unto them, nor serve them; for I am YHVH, the Lord thy God, I am a jealous God, visiting the iniquity of the fathers upon the children unto the third and fourth generation of them that hate Me; and showing mercy unto the thousandth generation of them that love Me.

3. Thou shalt not take the name of YHVH thy God in vain; for YHVH will not hold him guiltless that taketh His name in vain.

4. Remember the Sabbath day , to keep it holy. Six days shalt thou labor, and do all thy work; but the seventh day is a Sabbath unto YHVH thy God, in it thou shalt not do any manner of work, thou nor thy son, nor thy daughter, nor thy man-servant, nor thy maid servant, nor thy cattle, nor thy stranger that is within thy gates; for in six days YHVH made heaven and earth, the sea, and all that is in them, and rested on the seventh day; wherefore YHVH blessed the Sabbath day, and hallowed it.

5. Honor thy father and thy mother , that thy days may be long upon the land which YHVH thy God giveth thee.

6. Thou shalt not murder.

7. Thou shalt not commit adultery.

8. Thou shalt not steal.

9. Thou shalt not bear false witness against thy neighbor.

10. Thou shalt not covet thy neighbor's house, thou shalt not covet thy neighbor's wife, nor his man-servant, nor is maidservant, nor his ox, nor his ass, nor anything that is thy neighbor's.

See Exodus 20:2-14, Deuteronomy 5:6-18.

The 613 Laws

Take Two Tablets Daily

9

The Mandatory Commandments

The Israelite is required to [1]believe that YHVH exists, and to [2]acknowledge His unity, to [3]love, [4]fear, and [5]serve Him. He is also commanded to [6]cleave to Him (by associating with and imitating the wise) and to [7]swear only by His name. One must [8]imitate YHVH and [9]sanctify His name.

1. Ex 20:2
2. Deut 6:4
3. Deut 6:5
4. Deut 6:13
5. Ex 23:25; Deut 11:13; 6:13; 13:5
6. Deut 10:20
7. Deut 10:20
8. Deut 28:9
9. Lev 22:32

Torah

The Israelite must [10]recite the *Shema*[D] each morning and evening and [11]study the Torah [the first five books of Y'shua's Bible: Genesis, Exodus, Leviticus, Numbers and Deuteronomy] and teach it to others. He should bind *tefillin*[E] on his [12]head and [13]his arm. He should make [14]*tzizit*[F] for his garments and [15]fix a *mezuzah*[G] on his door. The people are to be [16]assembled every seventh year to hear the Torah read and [17]the king must write a special copy of the Torah for himself. [18]Every Israelite should have a Torah scroll. One should [19]praise YHVH after eating.

D *Shema*, Reading of, declaration of YHVH's unity and providence: "Hear O Israel, YHVH is our God, YHVH is One. Blessed be His Name, His kingdom is forever, and forever more." Contained in Deuteronomy 6:4-9, 11:13-212, Numbers 15:37-41.

E *Tefillin* (Hebrew for "phylacteries"), two black leather boxes fastened to leather straps, containing four portions of the Torah written on parchment (Exodus 13:1-10, 11-16; Deuteronomy 6:4-9;11;13-21). They are affixed on the forehead and the arm by the adult male Israelites during recital of morning prayers. They are not worn on the Sabbath and festivals, and on the Av 9 [A Post-Exillic Festival, it is traditional a day of mourning and fasting for the destruction of the temple in Jerusalem] they are worn during the afternoon service.

F *Zizit* or ziziyyot or Tzizit (fringes). The fringes at the four corners of the *Tallit* (four-cornered prayer shawl). The *Tallit* is usually white and made of wool, cotton, or silk, it is worn by male Israelites during morning prayers (except on Av 9, when it is worn at afternoon service) as well as throughout the Day of Atonement services.

G *Mezuzah* (doorpost), parchment scroll with selected Torah verses (Deuteronomy 6:4-9, 11:13-21) placed in a container and affixed to doorpost of rooms occupied by Israelites.

10. Deut 6:7
11. Deut 6:7
12. Deut 6:8
13. Deut 6:8
14. Num 15:38

15. Deut 6:9
16. Deut 31:12
17. Deut 17:18
18. Deut 31:19
19. Deut 8:10

Temple And The Priests

The Israelites should [20]build a Temple and [21]respect it. It must be [22]guarded at all times and the [23]Levites should perform their special duties in it. Before entering the Temple or participating in its service the priests [24]must wash their hands and feet; they must also [25]light the candelabrum daily. The priests are required to [26]bless Israel and to [27]set the shewbread and frankincense before the Ark. Twice daily they must [28]burn the incense on the golden altar. [29]Fire shall be kept burning on the altar continually and the [30]ashes should be removed daily. Ritually unclean persons must be [31]kept out of the Temple. Israel [32]should honor its priests, who must be [33]dressed in special priestly raiment. The priests should [34]carry the Ark on their shoulders, and the holy anointing oil [35]must be prepared according to its special formula. The priestly families should officiate in [36]rotation. In honor of certain dead close relatives the priests should [37]make themselves ritually unclean. The high priest may marry [38]only a virgin.

20. Ex 25:8
21. Lev 19:30
22. Num 18:4
23. Num 18:23
24. Ex 30:19
25. Ex 27:21
26. Num 6:23

27. Ex 25:30
28. Ex 30:7
29. Lev 21:8
30. Lev 6:3
31. Num 5:2
32. Lev 21:8
33. Ex 28:2

34. Num 7:9
35. Ex 30:31
36. Deut 18:6-8

37. Lev 21:2-3
38. Lev 21:13

Sacrifices

The [39]*tamid* [daily continual] *korban* [sacrifice] must be offered twice daily and the [40]high priest must also offer a meal-offering twice daily. A *musaf* [additional sacrifice] should be offered [41]every Sabbath, [42]on the first of every month, and [43]on each of the seven days of Passover. On the second day of Passover [44]a meal offering of the first barley must also be brought. On Shavuot [Hebrew for "Feast of Weeks or Pentecost"] a [45]*musaf* must be offered and [46]two loaves of bread as a wave offering. The additional sacrifice must also be made on [47]Rosh Ha-Shanah [New year] and [48]on the Day of Atonement when the [49]Avodah [service] must also be performed. On every day of the Festival of [50]Sukkot [Feast of Booths or Tabernacles] a *musaf* must be brought as well as on the [51]eight day thereof.

Every male Israelite should make [52]pilgrimage to the Temple three times a year and [53]appear there during the three pilgrim Festivals [Passover, Shavuot and Sukkot).

One should [54]rejoice on the Festivals.

On the 14th of Nisan [The day of preparation for the Passover meal.] one should [55]slaughter the paschal lamb and [56]eat of its roasted flesh on the night of the 15th [Passover meal]. Those who were ritually impure in Nisan should slaughter the paschal lamb on [57]the 14th of Iyyar and eat it with [58]*mazzah* [unleavened bread] and bitter herbs.

Trumpets should be [59]sounded when the festive

-34-

sacrifices are brought and also in times of tribulation.

Cattle to be sacrificed must be [60]at lest eight days old and [61]without blemish. All offerings must be [62]salted. It is a *mitzvah* [good deed] to perform the ritual of [63]burnt offering, [64]the sin offering, [65]the guilt offering, [66]the peace offering and the [67]meal offering.

Should the Sanhedrin [court] err in a decision its members [68]must bring a sin offering which offering must also be brought [69]by a person who has unwittingly transgressed a *Karet*[H] prohibition (i.e., one which, if done deliberately, would incur *Karet*). When in doubt as to whether one has transgressed such a prohibition a [70]"suspensive" guilt offering must be brought.

For [71]stealing or swearing falsely and for other sins of like nature, a guilt offering must be brought. In special circumstances the sin offering [72]can be according to one's means.

One must [73]confess one's sins before YHVH and repent for them.

A [74]man who has discharge from his body, and if he has a seminal discharge, or if he lies woman so that there is a seminal issue must bring a sacrifice; the woman also must bring a sacrifice. A [75] woman who has a discharge of blood, not at her menstrual impurity, when she becomes clean she bring a sacrifice; also a woman must also bring a sacrifice

---

H (Heavenly punishment for intentional sins). There are thirty-six sins for which the punishment is *kareis* (Spiritual Excision [removal] from the people of Israel). Punishment depends on the nature and severity of the sin and the sinner. Since *kareis* is heavenly punishment one can save himself from it through repentance.

^{76}after childbirth.

A leper must ^{77}bring a sacrifice after he has been cleansed.

One must ^{78}tithe one's cattle. The ^{79}first born males of clean (permitted) cattle are holy and must be sacrificed. The firstborn male of man must be ^{80}redeemed. The firstling (male) of the ass must be ^{81}redeemed; if not ^{82}its neck has to be broken.

Animals set aside as offerings ^{83}must be brought to Jerusalem without delay and ^{84}may be sacrificed only in the Temple. Offerings from outside the land of Israel ^{85}may also be brought to the Temple.

Sanctified animals ^{86}which have become blemished must be redeemed. A beast exchanged for an offering ^{87}is also holy.

The priests should eat ^{88}the remainder of the meal offering and ^{89}the flesh of sin and guilt offerings; but consecrated flesh which has become ^{90}ritually unclean or ^{91}which was not eaten within its appointed time must be burned.

39. Num 28:3		57. Num 9:11	
40. Lev 6:13		58. Num 9:11; Ex 12:8	
41. Num 28:9		59. Num 10:9-10	
42. Num 28:11		60. Lev 22:27	
43. Lev 23:36		61. Lev 22:21	
44. Lev 23:10		62. Lev 2:13	
45. Num 28:26-27		63. Lev 1:2	
46. Lev 23:17		64. Lev 6:18	
47. Num 29:1-2		65. Lev 7:1	
48. Num 28:26-27		66. Lev 3:1	
49. Lev 16		67. Lev 2:1,6,7	
50. Num 29:13		68. Lev 4:13	
51. Num 29:36		69. Lev 4:27	
52. Ex 23:14		70. Lev 5:17-18	
53. Ex 34:23		71. Lev 5:15, 21-15; Lev 19:20-21	
54. Deut 16:16		72. Lev 5:1-11	
55. Ex 12:6		73. Num 5:6-7	
56. Ex 12:8			

74. Lev 15:13-18
75. Lev 15:28-29
76. Lev 12:6
77. Lev 14:10
78. Lev 27:32
79. Ex 13:2
80. Ex 22:28;Num 18:15
81. Ex 34:20
82. Ex 13:13

83. Deut 12:5
84. Deut 14:14
85. Deut 12:26
86. Deut 12:15
87. Lev 27:33
88. Lev 6:9
89. Ex 29:33
90. Lev 7:19
91. Lev 7:17

VOWS

A Nazirite must [92]let his hair grow during the period of his separation. When that period is over he must [93]shave his head and bring his sacrifice.

A man must [94]honor his vows and his oaths which a judge can [95]annul only in accordance with the law.

92. Num 6:5
93. Num 6:18

94. Deut 23:24
95. Num 30:3

Ritual Purity

Anyone who touches [96]a carcass or [97]one of the eight species of reptiles becomes ritually unclean; food becomes unclean by [98]coming into contact with a ritually unclean object. Woman in their menstrual impurity [99]and those [100]lying-in after childbirth are ritually impure. A [101]leper, [102]leprous garment, and [103]a leprous house are all ritually unclean. A man having [104]a running issue is unclean, as is [105]semen. A woman suffering from [106]a running issue is also impure. A [107]human corpse is ritually unclean. The *mei niddah* [purification water] purifies [108]the unclean, but it makes the clean ritually impure. It is a *mitzvah* to become ritually clean [109]by ritual immersion. To become cleansed of leprosy one [110]must follow the specified procedure and also [111]shave off all of one's hair. Until cleansed the leper [112]must be bareheaded with clothing in disarray so as to be easily distinguishable.

The ashes of [113]the red heifer are to be used in the process of ritual purification.

96. Lev 11:18,24	105. Lev 15:16
97. Lev 11:29-31	106. Lev 15:19
98. Lev 11:34	107. Num 19:14
99. Lev 15:19	108. Num 19:13,2
100. Lev 12:2	109. Lev 15:16
101. Lev13:3	110. Lev 14:2
102. Lev 13:51	111. Lev 14:9
103. Lev 14:44	112. Lev 13:45
104. Lev 15:2	113. Num 19:2-9

Donations To The Temple

If a person [114]undertakes to give his own value to the Temple he must do so. Should a man declare [115]an unclean beast, [116]a house, or [117]a field as a donation to the Temple, he must give its value in money as fixed by the priest. If one unwittingly derives benefit from Temple property [118]full restitution plus a fifth must be made.

The fruit of [119]the fourth year's growth of trees is holy and may be eaten only in Jerusalem. When you reap your fields you must leave [120]the corners, [121]the gleanings, [122]the forgotten sheaves, [123]the misformed bunches of grapes and [124]the gleanings of the grapes for the poor.

The first fruits must be [125]separated and brought to the Temple and you must also [126]separate the *terumah* [great heave offering] and give it to the priests. You must give [127] one tithe of your produce to the Levites and separate [128]a second tithe which is to be eaten only in Jerusalem. The Levites [129]must give a tenth of their tithe to the priests.

In the third and sixth years of the seven year cycle you should [130]separate a tithe for the poor instead of the second tithe. A declaration [131]must be recited when separating the various tithes and [132]when bringing the first fruits to the Temple.

The first portion of the [133]dough must be given to the priest.

114.	Lev 27:2-8	125.	Ex 23:19
115.	Lev 27:11-12	126.	Deut 18:4
116.	Lev 27:14	127.	Lev 27:30;
117.	Lev 27:16,22,23		Num 18:24
118.	Lev 5:16	128.	Deut 14:22
119.	Lev 19:24	129.	Num 18:26
120.	Lev 19:9	130.	Deut 14:28
121.	Lev 19:9	131.	Deut 26:13
122.	Deut 24:19	132.	Deut 26:5
123.	Lev 19:10	133.	Num 15:20
124.	Lev 19:10		

The Sabbatical Year

In the *shemittah* [seventh year] everything that grows is [134]ownerless and available to all; the fields [135]must lie fallow and you may not till the ground. You must [136]sanctify the Jubilee year (50th) and on the day of Atonement in that year [137]you must sound the *shofar* [trumpet] and set all Hebrew slaves free. In the Jubilee year all land is to be [138]returned to its ancestral owners and, generally, in a walled city [139]the seller has the right to buy back a house within a year of the sale.

Starting from entry into the land of Israel, the years of the Jubilee must be [140]counted and announced yearly and septennially.

In the seventh year [141]all debts are annulled but [142]one may exact a debt owed by a foreigner.

134. Ex 23:11
135. Ex 34:21
136. Lev 25:10
137. Lev 25:9
138. Lev 25:24

139. Lev 25:29
140. Lev 25:8
141. Deut 15:3
142. Deut 15:3

Concerning Animals For Consumption

When you slaughter an animal you must [143]give the priest his share as you must also give him [144]the first of the fleece. When a man makes a *herem* [a special vow] you must [145]distinguish between that which belongs to the Temple (i.e. when YHVH's name was mentioned in the vow) and between that which goes to the priests. To be fit for consumption, beast and fowl must be [146]slaughtered according to the law and if they are not of a domesticated species [147]their blood must be covered with earth after slaughter.

Set the parent bird [148]free when taking the nest. Examine [149]beast, [150]fowl, [151]locust and [152]fish to determine whether they are permitted for consumption.

143. Deut 18:3
144. Deut 18:4
145. Lev 27:21,28
146. Deut 12:21
147. Lev 17:13

148. Deut 22:7
149. Lev 11:12
150. Deut 14:11
151. Lev 11:21
152. Lev 11:19

Festivals

The Sanhedrin should [153]sanctify the first day of every month and reckon the years and the seasons.

You must [154] rest on the Sabbath day and [155]declare it holy at its onset and termination. On the 14th of Nisan [156]remove all leaven from your ownership and on the night of the 15th [157]relate the story of the exodus from Egypt; on that night [158]you must also eat *mazzah.* On the [159]first and [160]seventh days of Passover you must rest. Starting from the day of the first sheaf (16th of Nisan) you shall [161]count 49 days. You must rest on [162]Shavuot, and on [163]Yom Teruah (Day of Blowing, or Feast of Trumpets); on the Day of Atonement you must [164]fast and [165]rest. You must also rest on [166]the first and [167]the eight day of Sukkot during which festival you shall [168]dwell in booths and [169]take the four species. On Yom Teruah [170]you are to hear the sound of the *shofar.*

153. Ex 12:2; Deut 16:1	162. Lev 23
154. Ex 23:12	163. Lev 23:24
155. Ex 20:8	164. Lev 16:29
156. Ex 12:15	165. Lev 16:29,31
157. Ex 13:8	166. Lev 23:35
158. Ex 12:18	167. Lev 23:36
159. Ex 12:16	168. Lev 23:42
160. Ex 12:16	169. Lev 23:40
161. Lev 23:35	170. Num 29:1

Community

Every male should [171]give half a shekel to the Temple annually.

You must [172]obey a prophet and [173]set a king over

you whom YHVH, the Lord your God appoints. You must also [174]obey the Sanhedrin; in the case of division, [175]yield to the majority. Judges and officials shall be [176]be appointed in every town and they shall judge the people [176]impartially.

Whoever is aware of evidence [178]must come to court to testify. Witnesses shall be [179]examined thoroughly and, if found to be false, [180]shall have done to them what they intended to do to the accused.

When a person is found murdered and the murder is unknown the ritual of [181]decapitating the heifer must be performed.

Six cities of refuge should be [182]established. The Levites, who have no ancestral share in the land, shall [183]be given cities to live in.

You must [184]build a fence around your roof and remove potential hazards from your home.

171.	Ex 30:12-13	178.	Lev 5:1
172.	Deut 18:15	179.	Deut 13:15
173.	Deut 17:15	180.	Deut 19:19
174.	Deut 17:11	181.	Deut 21:4
175.	Ex 23:2	182.	Deut 19:3
176.	Deut 16:18	183.	Num 35:2
177.	Lev 19:15	184.	Deut 22:8

Idolatry

Idolatry and its appurtenances [185]must be destroyed, and a city which has become perverted must be [186]treated according to the law. You are commanded to [187]destroy the seven Canaanite nations, and [188]to blot out the memory of Amalek, and [189]to remember what they did to Israel.

185. Deut 12:2; 7:5	186. Deut 13:17

187. Deut 20:17   189. Deut 25:17
188. Deut 25:19

War

The regulations for wars other than those commanded in the Torah [190]are to be observed and a priest should be [191]appointed for special duties in times of war. The military camp must be [192]kept in a sanitary condition. To this end, every soldier must be [193]equipped with the necessary implements.

190. Deut 20:11-12   192. Deut 23:14-15
191. Deut 20:2   193. Deut 23:14

Social

Stolen property must be [194]restored to its owner. Give [195]charity to the poor. When a Hebrew slave goes free the owner must [196]give him gifts. Lend to [197]the poor without interest; to the foreigner you may [198]lend at interest. Restore [199]a pledge to its owner if he needs it. Pay the worker his wages [200]on time; [201]permit him to eat of the produce with which he is working. You must [202]help an animal in distress when necessary, and also [203]help raise up your countryman's if it has fallen down. Lost property [204]must be restored to its owner. You are required [205]to reprove the sinner but you must [206]love your fellow man as yourself. You are commanded [207]to love the proselyte. Your weights and measures [208]must be accurate.

194. Lev 5:23   196. Deut 15:14
195. Deut 15:8;   197. Ex 22:24
    Lev 25:35-36   198. Deut 25:19

-43-

199. Deut 24:13; Ex 22:25	204. Deut 22:1; Ex 23:4
200. Deut 24:15	205. Lev 19:17
201. Deut 23:25-26	206. Lev 19:18
202. Ex 23:5	207. Deut 10:19
203. Deut 22:4-5	208. Lev 19:36

Family

Respect the [209]wise, [210]honor and [211]fear your parents.

You should [212]perpetuate the human race by marrying [213]according to the law. A bridegroom is to [214]rejoice with his bride for one year. Male children must [215]be circumcised. Should a man die childless his brother must either [216]marry his widow or [217]release her *(halizah)*. He who violates a virgin must [218]marry her and may never divorce her. If a man unjustly accuses his wife of premarital promiscuity [219]he shall be flogged, and may never divorce her. The seducer [220]must be punished according to the law. The female captive must be [221]treated in accordance with her special regulations. Divorce can be executed [222]only by means of a written document. A woman suspected of adultery [223]has to submit to the required test.

209. Lev 19:32	216. Deut 25:5
210. Ex 20:12	217. Deut 25:9
211. Lev 19:3	218. Deut 22:29
212. Gen 1:28	219. Deut 22:18-19
213. Deut 24:1	220. Ex 22:15-23
214. Deut 24:5	221. Deut 21:11
215. Gen 17:10;	222. Deut 24:1
Lev 12:3	223. Num 5-15-27

Judicial

When required by the law [224]you must administer the punishment of flogging and you must [225]exile the unwitting homicide. Capital punishment shall be by [226]the sword, [227]strangulation, [228]fire, or [229]stoning, as specified. In some cases the body of the executed [230]shall be hanged, but it [231]must be brought to burial the same day.

224. Deut 25:2	228. Lev 20:14
225. Num 35:25	229. Deut 22:24
226. Ex 21:20	230. Deut 21:22
227. Ex 21:16	231. Deut 21:23

Slaves

Hebrew slaves [232]must be treated according to the special laws for them. The master should [233]marry his Hebrew maidservant or [234]redeem her. The alien slave [235]must be treated according to the regulations applying to him.

232. Ex 21:2	234. Ex 21:8
233. Ex 21:8	235. Lev 25:46

Torts

The applicable law must be administered in the case of injury caused by [236]a person, [237]an animal or [238]pit. Thieves [239]must be punished. You must render judgement in cases of [240]trespass by cattle, [241]arson, [242]embezzlement by an unpaid guardian and in claims against [243]a paid guardian, a hirer, or [244]a borrower. Judgement must also be rendered in disputes arising out of [245]sales, [246]inheritance and [247]when goods are recovered but the thief is not caught. You are required to [248]rescue the persecuted even if it means killing his oppressor.

236. Ex 21:18
237. Ex 21:28
238. Ex 21:33-34
239. Ex 21:37-22:3
240. Ex 22:4
241. Ex 22:5
242. Ex 22:6-8

243. Ex 22:9-12
244. Ex 22:13
245. Lev 25:14
246. Num 27:8
247. Ex 22:8
248. Deut 25:12

10

Prohibitions

Idolatry And Related Practices

It is [1]forbidden to believe in the existence of any but YHVH, the One God. You may not make images [2]for yourself or [3]for others to worship or for [4]any other purpose.

You must not worship anything but YHVH, either in [5]the manner prescribed for His worship or [6]in its own manner of worship.

Do not sacrifice [7]children to Molech.

You may not [8]practice necromanaacy or [9]resort to "familiar spirits" neither should you take idolatry or its mythology [10]seriously.

It is forbidden to construct a [11]pillar or [12]dais even for the worship of YHVH or to [13]plant trees in the Temple.

You may not [14]swear by idols or instigate an idolater to do so, nor may you encourage or persuade any [15]non-Israelite or [16]Israelite to worship idols.

You must not [17]listen to or love anyone who

disseminates idolatry nor [18]should you withhold yourself from hating him. Do not [19]pity such a person. If somebody tries to convert you to idolatry [20]do not defend him or [21]conceal the fact.

It is forbidden to [22]drive any benefit from the ornaments of idols. You may not [23]rebuild that which has been destroyed as a punishment for idolatry nor may you [24]have any benefit from its wealth. Do not [25]use anything connected with idols or idolatry.

It is forbidden [26]to prophecy in the name of idols or prophecy [27]falsely in the name of YHVH. Do not listen to the one who prophesies for idols in the name of YHVH. Do not [28]listen to the one who prophesies for idols and do not [29]fear the false prophet or hinder his execution.

You must not [30]imitate the ways of idolators or practice their custom; [31]divination, [32]soothsaying, [33]enchanting, [34]sorcery, [35]charming, [36]consulting ghosts or [37]familiar spirits and [38]necromancy are forbidden. Women must not [39]wear male clothing nor men [40]that of women. Do not [41]tattoo yourself in the manner of the idolators.

You may not wear [42]garments made of both wool and linen nor round off the side-growth of your [43]head nor harm the edges of your [44]beard. Do not [45]lacerate yourself over your dead.

1. Ex 20:3	10. Lev 19:4
2. Ex 20:4	11. Deut 16:22
3. Lev 19:4	12. Lev 20:1
4. Ex 20:20	13. Deut 16:21
5. Ex 20:5	14. Ex 23:14
6. Ex 20:5	15. Ex 23:13
7 . Lev 18:21	16. Deut 13:12
8. Lev 19:31	17. Deut 13:9
9. Lev 19:31	18. Deut 13:9

19. Deut 13:9
20. Deut 13:9
21. Deut 13:9
22. Deut 7:25
23. Deut 13:17
24. Deut 13:18
25. Deut 7:26
26. Deut 18:20
27. Deut 18:20
28. Deut 13:3-4
29. Deut 18:22
30. Lev 20:23
31. Lev 19:26; Deut 18:10
32. Deut 18:10
33. Deut 18:10-11;

Deut 10:26
34. Deut 18:10-11
35. Deut 18:10-11
36. Deut 18:10-11
37. Deut 18:10-11
38. Deut 18:10-11
39. Deut 22:5
40. Deut 22:11
41. Lev 19:28
42. Deut 22:11
43. Lev 19:27
44. Lev 19:27
45. Deut 16:1; 14:1;
    Lev 19:28

Prohibitions Resulting From Historical Events

It is forbidden to return to Egypt to [46]dwell there permanently or to [47]indulge in impure thoughts or sights. You may not [48]make pact with the seven Canaanite nations or [49]save the life of any member of them. Do not [50]show mercy to idolators, [51]permit them to dwell in the land of Israel or [52]intermarry with them. A Israelite shall not [53]marry an Ammonite or Moabite but should not refuse (for reasons of genealogy alone) [54]a descendent of Esau or [55]an Egyptian who are proselytes. It is prohibited to [56]make peace with the Ammonite or Moabite nations.

The [57]destruction of fruit trees even in times of war is forbidden as is wanton waste at any time. Do not [58]fear the enemy and do not [59]forget the evil done by Amalek.

46. Deut 17:16
47. Num 15:39
48. Ex 23:32

49. Deut 20:16
50. Deut 7:2
51. Ex 23:33

52. Deut 7:3	56. Deut 23:7
53. Deut 23:4	57. Deut 20:19
54. Deut 23:8	58. Deut 25:19
55. Deut 23:8	59. Deut 25:19

Blasphemy

You must not [60]blaspheme the Holy Name, [61] break an oath made by it, [62]take it in vain or [63]profane It. Do not [64]try YHVH. your Lord. You may not [65]erase YHVH's name from the holy texts or destroy institutions devoted to His worship. Do not [66]allow the body of one hanged to remain so overnight.

60. Lev 24:16; Ex 22:27	64. Deut 6:16
61. Lev 19:12	65. Deut 12:4
62. Ex 20:7	66. Deut 21:23
63. Lev 22:32	

Temple

Be not [67]lax in guarding the Temple.

The high priest must not enter the Temple [68]indiscriminately; a priest with a physical blemish may not [69]enter there at all or [70]serve in the sanctuary and even if the blemish is of a temporary nature he may not [71]participate in the service there until it has passed.

The Levites and priest must not [72]interchange in their functions. Intoxicated persons may not [73]enter the sanctuary or teach the Law. It is forbidden for [74]non-priests, [75]unclean priests or [76]priests who have performed the necessary ablution but are still within the time limit of their uncleanness to serve in the Temple. No unclean person may enter [77]the Temple or

[78]the Temple Mount.

The altar must not be made of [79]hewn stones nor may the ascent to it be by [80]steps. The fire on it may not be [81]extinguished nor may any other but the specified incense be [82]burned on the golden altar. You may not [83]manufacture oil with the same ingredients and in the same proportions as the anointing oil which itself [84]may not be misused. Neither may you[65]compound incense with the same ingredients and in the same proportions as that burnt on the altar. You must [86]remove the staves from the Ark, [87]remove the breastplate from the ephod or [88]make any incision in the upper garment of the high priest.

67. Num 18:5	78. Deut 23:11
68. Lev 16:2	79. Ex 20:25
69. Lev 21:23	80. Ex 20:26
70. Lev 21:17	81. Lev 6:6
71. Lev 21:18	82. Ex 30:9
72. Num 189:3	83. Ex 30:32
73. Lev 10:9-11	84. Ex 30:32
74. Num 18:4	85. Ex 30:37
75. Lev 22:2	86. Ex 25:15
76. Lev 21:6	87. Ex 28:28
77. Num 5:3	88. Ex 28:32

Sacrifices

It is forbidden to [89]offer sacrifices or [90]slaughter consecrated animals outside the Temple. You may not [91]sanctify, [92]slaughter, [93]sprinkle the blood of, or [94]burn the inner parts of a blemished animal even if the blemish is [95]of a temporary nature and even if it is [96]offered by Gentiles. It is forbidden to [97]inflict a blemish on an animal consecrated for sacrifice.

Leaven or honey may not [98]be offered on the altar,

neither may [99]anything unsalted. An animal received as the hire of a harlot or as the price of a dog [100]may not be offered.

Do not [101]kill an animal and its young on the same day.

It is forbidden to use [102]olive oil or [103]frankincense in the sin offering or [104,105,]in the *sotah* [jealousy offering]. You may not [105]substitute sacrifices even [107]from one category to the other. You may not [108]redeem the firstborn of permitted animals. It is forbidden to [119]sell the tithe of the herd or [110]sell or [111]redeem a field consecrated by the *herem* [Hebrew for "excommunication"] vow.

When you slaughter a bird for a sin offering you may not [112]split its head.

It is forbidden to [113]work with or [114]to shear a consecrated animal. You must not slaughter the paschal [passover] lamb [115]while there is still leaven about; nor may you leave overnight [116]those parts that are to be offered up or [117]to be eaten.

You may not leave any part of the festival offering [118]until the third day or any part of [119]the second paschal lamb or [120]the thanksgiving offering until the morning.

It is forbidden to break a bone of the [121]first or [122]the second paschal lamb or [123]to carry their flesh out of the house where it is being eaten. You must not [124]allow the remains of the meal offering to become leaven. It is also forbidden to eat the paschal lamb [125]raw or sodden or allow [126]an alien resident, [127]an uncircumcised person or an [128]apostate to eat of it.

A ritually unclean person [129]must not eat of holy things nor may [130]holy things which have become unclean be eaten. Sacrificial meat [131]which is left after the time-limit or [132]which was slaughtered with wrong intentions must not be eaten. The heave offering must not be eaten by a [133]non-priest, [134]a priest sojourner or hired worker, [135]an uncircumcised person, or [136]an unclean priest. The daughter of a priest who is married to a non-priest may not [137]eat of holy things.

The meal offering of the priest [138]must not be eaten, neither may [139]the flesh of the sin offerings sacrificed within the sanctuary or [140]consecrated animals which have become blemished.

You may not eat the second tithe of [141]corn, [142]wine, or [143]oil or [144]unblemished firstlings outside Jerusalem. The priests may not eat the [145]sin-offerings or the trespass-offerings outside the Temple court or of the burnt-offering at all. The lighter sacrifices [147]may not be eaten before the blood has been sprinkled. A non-priest may not [148]eat of the holiest sacrifices and a priest [149]may not eat the first-fruits outside the Temple courts.

One may not eat [150]the second tithe while in state of impurity or [151]in mourning; its redemption money [152]may not be used for anything other than food and a drink.

You must not [153]eat untithed produce or [154]change the order of separating the various tithes.

Do not [155]delay payment of offerings—either freewill or obligatory—and do not [156]come to the Temple on the pilgrim festivals without an offering.

Do not [157]break your word.

89. Deut 12:13	94. Lev 22:22
90. Lev 17:3-4	95. Deut 17:1
91. Lev 22:20	96. Lev 22:25
92. Lev 22:22	97. Lev 22:21
93. Lev 22:24	98. Lev 2:11

99. Lev 2:13		129. Lev 12:4	
100. Deut 23:19		130. Lev 7:19	
101. Lev 22:28		131. Lev 19:6-8	
102. Lev 5:11		132. Lev 7:18	
103. Lev 5:11		133. Lev 22:10	
104. Num 5:15		134. Lev 22:10	
105. Num 5:15		135. Lev 22:10	
106. Lev 27:10		136. Lev 22:10	
107. Lev 27:26		137. Lev 22:12	
108. Num 18:17		138. Lev 6:16	
109. Lev 27:33		139. Lev 6:23	
110. Lev 27:28		140. Deut 14:3	
111. Lev 27:28		141. Deut 12:17	
112. Lev 5:8		142. Deut 12:17	
113. Deut 15:19		143. Deut 12:17	
114. Deut 15:19		144. Deut 12:17	
115. Ex 34:25		145. Deut 12:17	
116. Ex 23:10		146. Deut 12:17	
117. Ex 12:10		147. Deut 12:17	
118. Deut 16:4		148. Deut 12:17	
119. Num 9:13		149. Ex 29:33	
120. Lev 22:30		150. Deut 26:14	
121. EX 12:46		151. Deut 26:14	
122. Num 9:12		152. Deut 26:14	
123. Ex 12:46		153. Lev 22:15	
124. Lev 6:10		154. Ex 22:28	
125. Ex 12:9		155. Deut 32:22	
126. Ex 12:45		156. Ex 23:15	
127. Ex 12:48		157. Num 30:3	
128. Ex 12:43			

Priests

A priest may not marry [158]a harlot, [159]a woman who has been profaned from the priesthood, or [160]a divorcee, the high priest must not [161]marry a widow or [162]take one as a concubine. Priests may not enter the sanctuary with [163]overgrown hair of the head or [164]with torn clothing; they must not [165]leave the courtyard during the Temple service. An ordinary priest may not render himself [166]ritually impure except for those relatives specified, and the high priest should not become impure [167]for anybody in [168]in any way.

The tribe of Levi shall have no part in [169]the division of the land of Israel or [170]in the spoils of war.

It is forbidden [171]to make oneself bald as a sign of mourning for one's dead.

158. Lev 21:7	165. Lev 10:7
159. Lev 21:7	166. Lev 21:1
160. Lev 21:7	167. Lev 21:11
161. Lev 21:14	168. Lev 21:11
162. Lev 21:15	169. Deut 18:1
163. Lev 10:6	170. Deut 18:1
164. Lev 10:6	171. Deut 14:1

Dietary Laws

An Israelite may not eat [172]unclean cattle, [173]unclean fish, [174]unclean fowl, [175] creeping things that fly, [176]creatures that creep on the ground, [177]reptiles, [178]worms found on fruit or produce, or [179]any detestable creature.

An animal that has died naturally [180]is forbidden for consumption as is [181]a torn or mauled animal. One must not eat [182]any limb taken from a living animal. Also prohibited is [183]*gid ha nasheh* [the sinew of the thigh] as is [184]blood and [185]*helev* [certain types of fat]. It is forbidden [186]to cook meat together with milk or [187]eat of such a mixture. It is also forbidden to eat [188]of an ox condemned to stoning (even should it have been properly slaughtered).

One may not eat [189]bread made of new corn or the new corn itself either [190]roasted of [191]green, before the 24*omer* offering has been brought on the 16th of Nisan. You may not eat [192] *orlah* [fruit of trees during first three years after planting] or [193] the growth of mixed planting in the vineyard.

Any use of [194] wine libations to idols is prohibited, as is [195] gluttony and drunkenness. One may not eat anything on [196] the Day of Atonement. During Passover it is forbidden to eat [197] *hamez* [leaven] or [198] anything containing an admixture of such. This is also forbidden [199] after the middle of the 14th of Nisan (the day before Passover). During Passover no leaven may be [200] seen of [201] found in your possession.

172. Deut 14:7	188. Ex 21:28
173. Lev 11:11	189. Lev 23:14
174. Lev 11:11	190. Lev 23:14
175. Deut 14:19	191. Lev 23:14
176. Lev 11:41	192. Lev 19:23
177. Lev 11:44	193. Deut 22:9
178. Lev 11:42	194. Deut 32:38
179. Lev 11:43	195. Lev 19:26;
180. Deut 14:21	Deut 21:20
181. Ex 22:30	196. Lev 23:29
182. Deut 12:23	197. Ex 13:3
183. Gen 32:33	198. Ex 13:20
184. Lev 7:26	199. Deut 16:3
185. Lev 7:23	200. Ex 13:7
186. Ex 23:19	201. Ex 12:19
187. Ex 34:26	

Nazirites

A Nazirite may not drink [202] wine or any beverage made from grapes; he may not eat [203] fresh grapes, [204] dried grapes, [205] grape seeds or [206] grape peel. He may not render himself [207] ritually impure for his dead nor may he [208] enter a tent in which there is a corpse. He must not [209] shave his hair.

202. Num 6:3	203. Num 6:3

204. Num 6:3	207. Num 6:7
205. Num 6:4	208. Lev 21:11
206. Num 6:4	209. Num 6:5

Agriculture

It is forbidden [210]to reap the whole of a field without leaving the corners for the poor; it is also forbidden to [211]gather up the ears of corn that fall during reaping or to harvest [212]the misformed clusters of grapes, or [213]the grapes that fall or to [214]return to take a forgotten sheaf.
You must not [215]sow different species of seed together or [216]corn in a vineyard; it is also forbidden to [217]crossbreed different species of animal or [218]work with two different species yoked together.
You must not [219]muzzle an animal working in a field to prevent it from eating.
It is forbidden to [220]till the earth[221]to prune tree, [222]to reap (in the usual manner) produce or [223]fruit which has grown without cultivation in the *shemittah* [seventh year]. One may also not [224]till the earth or prune trees in the Jubilee, when it is also forbidden to harvest [in the usual manner] [225]produce or [226]fruit that has grown without cultivation.
One may not [227]sell one's landed inheritance in the land of Israel permanently or [228]change the lands of the Levites or [229]leave the Levites without support.

210. Lev 23:22	219. Deut 25:4
211. Lev 19:9	220. Lev 25:4
212. Lev 19:10	221. Lev 25:4
213. Lev 19:10	222. Lev 25:5
214. Deut 24:19	223. Lev 25:5
215. Lev 19:19	224. Lev 25:11
216. Deut 22:9	225. Lev 25:11
217. Lev 19:19	226. Lev 25:11
218. Deut 22:10	227. Lev 25:23

228. Lev 25:33   229. Duet 12:19

Loans, Business, And The Treatment of Slaves

It is forbidden to [230]demand repayment of a loan after the seventh year; you may not however, [231]refuse to lend to the poor because that year is approaching. Do no [232]deny charity to the poor or [233]send a Hebrew slave away empty-handed when he finishes his period of service. Do not [234]dun you debtor when you know that he cannot pay. It is forbidden [235]to lend to or [236]borrow from another Israelite at interest or [237]participate in an agreement involving interest either as a guarantor, witness, or writer of the contract.

Do not [238]delay payment of wages.

You may not [239]take a pledge from a debtor by violence, [240]keep a poor man's pledge when he needs it, [241]take any pledge from a widow or [242]from any debtor if he earns his living with it.

Kidnaping [243]a Israelite is forbidden.

Do not [244]steal or [245]rob by violence. Do not [246]remove a landmarker or [247]defraud.

It is forbidden [248]to deny receipt of a loan or a deposit or [249]to swear falsely regarding another man's property.

You must not [250]deceive anybody in business. You may not [251]mislead a man even verbally. It is forbidden to harm the stranger among you [252]verbally or [253]do him injury in trade.

You may not [254]return or [255]otherwise take advantage of, a slave who has fled to the land of Israel from his master, even if his master is an Israelite.

Do not [256]afflict the widow or the orphan. You may not [257]misuse or [258]sell a Hebrew slave; do not [259]treat him cruelly or [260]allow a heathen to mistreat him. You must not [261]sell your Hebrew maidservant or, if you marry her, [262]withhold food, clothing, and conjugal rights from her. You must not [263]sell a female captive or [264]treat her as a slave.

Do not [265]covet another man's possessions even if you are willing to pay for them. Even [266]the desire alone is forbidden.

A worker must not [267]cut down standing corn during his work or [268]take more fruit than he can eat.

One must not [269]turn away from a lost article which is to be returned to its owner nor may you [270]refuse to help a man or an animal which is collapsing under its burden.

It is forbidden to [271]defraud with weights and measures or even [272]to possess inaccurate weights.

230. Deut 15:2	250. Lev 25:14
231. Deut 15:9	251. Lev 25:17
232. Deut 15:7	252. Ex 22:20
233. Deut 15:13	253. Ex 22:20
234. Ex 22:25-27	254. Deut 23:16
235. Lev 25:37	255. Deut 23:17
236. Deut 23:20	256. Ex 22:21
237. Ex 22:24	257. Lev 25:39
238. Lev 19:13	258. Lev 25:42
239. Deut 24:10	259. Lev 25:43
240. Deut 24:12	260. Lev 25:53
241. Deut 24:17	261. Ex 21:8
242. Deut 24:6	262. Ex 21:10
243. Ex 20:13	263. Deut 21:14
244. Lev 19:11	264. Deut 21:14
245. Lev 19:13	265. Ex 20:17
246. Deut 19:14	266. Deut 5:18
247. Lev 19:13	267. Deut 23:26
248. Lev 19:11	268. Deut 23:25
249. Lev 19:11	269. Deut 22:3

270. Ex 23:5   272. Deut 25:13
271. Lev 19:35

Justice

A judge must not [273]perpetrate injustice, [274]accept bribes or be [275]partial or [276]afraid. He may [277]not favor the poor or [278]discriminate against the wicked; he should not [279]pity the condemned or [280]pervert the judgement of strangers or orphans.

It is forbidden to [281]hear one litigant without the other being present.

A capital case cannot be decided by [282]a majority of one.

A judge should not [283]accept a colleague's opinion unless he is convinced of its correctness; it is forbidden to [284]appoint as a judge someone who is ignorant of the law.

Do not [285]give false testimony or accept [286]testimony from a wicked person or from [287]relatives of a person involved in the case. It is forbidden to pronounce judgement [288]on the basis of the testimony of one witness.

Do not [283]murder.

You must not convict on [290]circumstantial evidence alone.

A witness [291]must not sit as a judge in capital cases.

You must not [292]execute anybody without due and proper trial and conviction.

Do not [293]pity or spare the pursuer.

Punishment is not to be inflicted for [294]an act committed under duress.

Do not accept ransom [295]for a murderer or [296]a manslayer.

Do not [297]hesitate to save another person from

danger and do not [298]leave a stumbling block in the way or [299]mislead another person by giving wrong advice.

It is forbidden [300]to administer more than the assigned number of lashes to the guilty.

Do not [301]tell tales or [302]bear hatred in your heart. It is forbidden to [303]shame a fellow Israelite, [304]to bear a grudge or [305]to take revenge.

Do not [306]take the mother when you take young birds.

It is forbidden to [307]shave a leprous scale or [308]remove other signs of that affliction. It is forbidden [309]to cultivate a valley in which a slain body was found and which subsequently the ritual of *eglah arufah* [breaking the heifer's neck] was not performed.

Do not [310]suffer a witch to live.

Do not [311]force a bridegroom to perform military service during the first year of his marriage. It is forbidden to [312]rebel against the transmitters of the tradition or to [313]add or [314]detract from the precepts of the law.

Do not curse [315]a judge, [316]a ruler or [317]any Israelite. Do not [318]curse or [319]strike a parent.

It is forbidden to [320]work on the Sabbath or [321]walk further than the *eruv* [permitted limits]. You may not [322]inflict punishment on the Sabbath.

It is forbidden to work on [323]the first or [324]the seventh day of Passover, on [325]Shavuot, on [326]Rosh Ha-Shanah, on the [327]first and [328]eighth days of Sukkot and [329]on the Day of Atonement.

273. Lev 19:15
274. Ex 23:8
275. Lev 19:15
276. Deut 1:17
277. Lev 19:15
278. Ex 23:6
279. Deut 19:13
280. Deut 24:17
281. Ex 23:1
282. Ex 23:2

283. Ex 23:2
284. Deut 1:17
285. Ex 20:16
286. Ex 23:1
287. Deut 24:16
288. Deut 19:15
289. Ex 20:13
290. Ex 23:7
291. Num 35:30
292. Num 35:12
293. Deut 25:12
294. Deut 22:26
295. Num 35:31
296. Num 35:32
297. Lev 19:16
298. Deut 22:8
299. Lev 19:14
300. Deut 25:2-3
301. Lev 19:16
302. Lev 19:17
303. Lev 19:17
304. Lev 19:18
305. Lev 19:18
306. Deut 22:6

307. Lev 13:33
308. Deut 24:8
309. Deut 21:4-9
310. Ex 22:17
311. Deut 24:5
312. Deut 17:11
313. Deut 13:1
314. Deut 13:1
315. Ex 22:27
316. Ex 22:27
317. Lev 19:14
318. Ex 21:17
319. Ex 21:15
320. Ex 20:10
321. Ex 16:29
322. Ex 35:3
323. Ex 12:16
324. Ex 12:16
325. Lev 23:21
326. Lev 23:25
327. Lev 23:35
328. Lev 23:36
329. Lev 23:28

Incest And Other Forbidden Relationships

It is forbidden to enter into an incestuous relationship with one's [330]mother, [331]step-mother, [332]sister, [333]step-sister, [334]son's daughter, [335]daughter's daughter, [336]daughter, [337]any woman and her daughter, [338]any woman and her son's daughter, [339]any woman and her daughter's daughter, [340]father's sister, [341]mother's sister, [342]paternal uncle's wife, [343]daughter-in-law, [344]brother's wife and [345]wife's sister.

It is also forbidden to [346]have sexual relations with a woman in her menstrual impurity.

Do not [347]commit adultery.

It is forbidden for [348]a man or [349]a woman to have sexual intercourse with an animal.

Homosexuality [350]is forbidden, particularly with [351]one's father or [352]uncle.

It is forbidden to have [353]intimate physical contact (even without actual intercourse) with any of the women with whom intercourse is forbidden.

A *mamzer* [one born of a forbidden marriage nor any of his descendants] may not marry a female Israelite.

Harlotry [355]is forbidden.

A divorcee may not be[356]remarried to her first husband if, in the meanwhile, she had married another.

A childless widow may not [357]marry anybody other than her late husband's brother.

A man may not [358]divorce a wife whom he married after having raped her or [359]after having slandered her.

A eunuch may not [360]marry a female Israelite.

Castration [361]is forbidden.

330. Lev 18:7		346. Lev 18:19
331. Lev 18:8		347. Lev 18:20
332. Lev 18:9		348. Lev 18:23
333. Lev 18:11		349. Lev 18:23
334. Lev 18:10		350. Lev 18:22
335. Lev 18:10		351. Lev 18:7
336. Lev 18:10		352. Lev 18:14
337. Lev 18:17		353. Lev 18:6
338. Lev 18:17		354. Deut 23:3
339. Lev 18:17		355. Deut 23:18
340. Lev 18:12		356. Deut 24:4
341. Lev 18:13		357. Deut 25:5
342. Lev 18:14		358. Deut 22:29
343. Lev 18:15		359. Deut 22:19
344. Lev 18:16		360. Deut 23:2
345. Lev 18:18		361. Lev 22:24

The Monarchy

You may not [362]elect as king anybody who is not of the seed of Israel.

The king must not accumulate an excessive number of [363]horses, [364]wives, or [365]wealth.

362. Deut 17:15
363. Deut 17:16
364. Deut 17:17
365. Deut 17:17

Bibliography

The following is a partial listing of the writings that have been of use in the making of this book.

Ausubel, Nathan. The *Book of Jewish Knowledge*. New York, NY: Crown Publishers, 1964

Bacchiocchi, Samuel. *The Sabbath in the New Testament.* Berrian Springs, MI: University Printers, 1985.

Birnbaum, Philip. *A Book Of Jewish Concepts.* New York, NY: Hebrew Publishing Company, 1975.

Botkin, Daniel. *The Ghost of Marcion,* Jerusalem, Israel: First Fruits of Zion, 4/1994

Encyclopaedic Dictionary Of Judaica. Jerusalem, Israel: Keter Publihing House Ltd, 1974.

Encyclopedia Judaica. 16 volumes. Jerusalem, Israel: Keter Publishing House Ltd., 1972.

Holdcroft, Thomas L. *The Pentateuch.* Oakland, CA: Western Book Company, 1966.

House of David Heralds. Lakewood, NY (1988-91), White Stone, VA (1992-95, and Saint Cloud, FL (1996-2000): House of David, 1988-1995.

Isaacson, Ben. *Dictionary Of The Jewish Religion.* New York, NY. Bantam Books, 1979

Lamsa, George M. *The Holy Bible From Ancient Eastern Manuscripts,* Nashville, TN, A. J. Holman, 1968, 1984.

New International Version Study Bible. Grand Rapids, MI: Zondervan Bible Publishers, 1985.

The Jewish Encyclopedia. New York, NY: Funk and Wagnalls, 1903.

The New Encyclopaedia Britannica. 29 volumes. Chicago, IL: Encyclopaedia Britannica, Inc., 1985.

Vaughn, Curtis, ed. *26 Translations of the Holy Bible.* Atlanta: Mathis, 1985.

Wootten, Angus. *Restoring Israel's Kingdom.* Saint Cloud, FL: Key of David, 2000.

Wootten, Batya Ruth. *In Search of Israel.* Lakewood, NY: Destiny Image/House of David, 1988.

_____. *The Olive Tree of Israel.* White Stone, VA: House of David, 1992.

_____. *Who Is Israel? And Why You Need To Know.* Saint Cloud, FL: Key of David, 1998.

_____. *Who Is Israel? Enlarged Edition.* Saint Cloud, FL: Key of David, 2000.

Index

Angus Wootten

Angus Wootten, and his wife Batya, have discovered a key that unlocks latter-day prophecy! Years ago they saw the Scriptural truth about the two houses of Israel (Ephraim and Judah). They also saw that the God of Abraham, Isaac and Jacob said He would restore His Kingdom to a "united" and "sinless" house of Israel—over which the Greater Son of David (the Messiah) will rule forever.

They also realize that the restoration of the Kingdom to Israel requires that Ephraim understand his heritage and his God given missions.

In the Seventies, these pioneers of the faith founded the House of David, through which they created the first Messianic Materials Catalogue. However, they soon saw both the houses of Israel in Scripture, and they realized the need for Ephraim to discover the truth of his own Israelite roots.

For decades these two have worked to gather the lost sheep of the house of Israel, and to confirm to them that which the God of Israel is writing on their hearts.

Over the years the House of David became Messianic Israel Ministries, an organization that provides a supportive umbrella for the Messianic Israel Alliance and Key of David Publishing. These ministries produce challenging conferences, seminars, materials, and informative literature—including the *House of David Herald Newsletter*, the *Messianic Israel Herald Magazine*, books by Angus: *Restoring Israel's Kingdom* and Take Two Tablets Daily, and books by Batya: *In Search of Israel, The Olive Tree of Israel, The*

Star of David, Who Is Israel? And Why You Need To Know, Who Is Israel? Expanded Edition, Ephraim and Judah, Israel Revealed, and the forthcoming book, *Israel's Feasts And Their Fullness.*

Angus wrote *Take Two Tablets Daily* to help Believers deal with a dividing wall that exists between the two houses, Ephraim and Judah. Because, both houses of Israel have errant attitudes toward the Laws and Commandments of the Holy One of Israel.

Angus, a retired Army Colonel, is a visionary. His burning desire is to "Take the hill!" As a former military strategist he realizes the need for the troops (the armies of Israel) to keep their eye on their ultimate goal. With this thought in mind, he wrote his classic book, *Restoring Israel's Kingdom.* This inspiring book outlines not only the ultimate objective for all who love the God of Israel, it also details the plan for attaining that glorious goal!

The Woottens reside in the Orlando area. They have ten children, fourteen grandchildren, and one great grandchild.

Read their books and be blessed.

RESTORING ISRAEL'S
KINGDOM

by Angus Wootten

What was the last question Messiah Y'shua's disciples asked their Teacher as they stood on the Mount of Olives, knowing that He was about to depart? What mattered most to them?

As followers of Israel's Messiah, have we asked the question that mattered so much to the chosen twelve? With olive groves serving as a backdrop, these fathers of our faith asked the King of Israel, "Lord, is it at this time You are restoring the kingdom to Israel?" (Acts 1:6).

Why did Y'shua's disciples, who had been trained by Him for more than three years, ask this particular question? Could it be because He had taught them to pray to our Father in Heaven, "Thy Kingdom come, on earth, as it is in Heaven"? (Matthew 6:10).

Since we are a people dedicated to bringing Y'shua's Kingdom o this earth, we must not lose sight of the vision that burned in the hearts of His first disciples. As part of His "chosen people" (1 Peter 1:1; 2:9), we must not lose sight of what should be our ultimate goal.

But, have we forgotten this important goal, even as we have lost sight or our heritage as part Israel? Could we be part of Ephraim/Israel—those so long ago blinded to the truth of their Israelite roots? (Genesis 48:19; Hosea 1-2; 8:8; Amos 9:9).

Just as Judah is beginning to see the Messiah, is the veil likewise being lifted from our "partially blinded" Israelite eyes? Do we belong to Israel's "olive tree" in a greater way than we had previously imagined? (Isaiah 8:14; Romans 11:25; Jeremiah 31:18-19; 11:10,16; 2:18,21). Is that why we are feeling a longing in our hearts for something more? Do we now feel a hunger deep within because the "set time" to restore Israel's Kingdom is upon us? If so, are we prepared to work toward that goal?

Restoring Israel's Kingdom offers the following challenging chapters: Are You Prepared? — Can We Make A Difference — Learning the Lessons of History — A Brief History of Israel — Lessons Learned — The Voice of The People — Who Told You? — Who Is A Jew? A Look At Israel's Bloodline — Our Hope of Glory And The Mystery of The Gentiles — The Way of The Gentiles — Ephraim, Once Again A Mighty Man — Ephraim Should Know More About Judah — From Roman Roads To The World Wide Web — The Jubilee Generation — A Mandate For Ephraim — Restoring The Kingdom To Israel — The Messianic Vision — When Will Y'shua Return — Preparing For The Final Battle. Plus a helpful Index.

Don't miss this exciting book! It will help you keep your eye on the goal, which is, the restoration of the Kingdom to the restored house of Israel.

ISBN 1-886987-04-1, Paper, 304 pages, $14.95.

Another Great Book From Key of David Publishing

Distributed by— *unlocking your future...*

⑥MESSIANIC ISRAEL ⑥MINISTRIES

Write or Call For a FREE Catalog!!
PO Box 700217, Saint Cloud, FL 34770
1 800 829-8777, or visit the Marketplace at

Take Two Tablets Daily
The 10 Commandments and 613 Laws

by Angus Wootten

The 10 Commandments
and the 613 Laws

Angus Wootten

"You are trying to put me under the Law!"

This is a common cry from many Christians when presented with the Laws and Commandments of the God of Abraham, Isaac and Jacob.

Is the cry justified?

This invaluable book will help you to thoughtfully examine the laws the Holy One gave to His people through Moses. Read it and see that the Father's commandments were given for the physical and spiritual guidance of His people. His judgments and precepts were given, not to punish Israel, but to guide them, both as individuals and as a nation. They were given to help them become a strong, courageous, healthy and blessed people.

A handy guide, this work conveniently lists the 613 laws, divided into Mandatory Commandments and Prohibitions (according to Jewish custom), plus the Scripture verse(s) from which each law is derived.

Chapter titles: Under the Law? — Y'shua's Attitude Toward the Law — Our Need For Law And Order — YHVH's Law Or Man's Law? — Paul and the Law — Principles of the Protestant Reformation — What Should Our Attitude Be Toward the Law? — The Decalogue: The Ten Commandments.

YHVH's Word is medicine, and nothing is more symbolic of His Word than the two tablets on which He wrote His desires for us. Taken daily, these "Two Tablets" will give us life more abundantly. This reference book should be in every Believers library. It is a must read!

ISBN1-886987-06-8, Paper, 96 Informative pages, $4.95.

—Who Is—
Israel?
Enlarged Edition

by Batya Wootten

This phenomenal book is causing a stir—because it clarifies misunderstandings about Israel. The truth about "both the houses of Israel" (Isaiah 8:14) is causing a reformation in the Body of Messiah! Read this solution driven book and see the truth that is inspiring Believers everywhere!

Who is Israel? Why do *you* even need to know? Because knowing who you are and where you are going is vital to your relationship with the GOD of Israel.

You need to read this book because it will: Inspire and encourage you, even change your life — Help you discover your own Hebraic Heritage — Put your feet on the road to Zion. Read this Scriptural account of Israel and understand: Israel, the Church, the Bible — The mystery of the "fullness of the Gentiles" — The "blindness of 'Israel'" — The Father's master plan for Israel — This guidebook will explain why you: Feel something is "missing" in your life — Have an unexplainable love for Israel and Jewish people — Feel an urge to celebrate the feasts of Israel.

This handbook will help you to: Move from religion to relationship — Unmuddle the muddled doctrines of Christianity — Properly intercede for "all Israel" — Remove the stones from Israel's road home — Live the *Shema*, the heart of New Covenant faith — Fulfill the latter-day desires of the Father's heart. The Biblical truths unveiled in this volume will help: Put an end to "Christian" anti-Semitism —

Heal divisions in the Body of Messiah — Cure the plague of "Believer's Boredom" — Relieve "rootlessness" in non-Jews who love "Israel." This book: Leads us back to our First Love — Lifts up Messiah Y'shua — Gives Him His proper place — Shows how He is the epitome of all that is "Israel." The revelation that unfolds on these pages will enrich your relationship with the Holy One of Israel; it will lead Jewish and non-Jewish Believers (Judah and Ephraim) to become the promised "one new man." Read them and be blessed.

This enlightening book includes a Foreword and Introduction, plus the following encouraging chapters: Believing What Abraham Believed — Israel: A Blessing — Jacob's Firstborn Heir — Ephraim: A Profile — Yankees and Rebels — LoAmmi: Not A People — Many Israels, One Israel — A Priceless Gift — Chosen To Choose — The Blood, The Redeemer, And Physical Israel — Literal or Spiritual? — Israel: A Mystery Until — "Holey" Doctrines — More Tattered Theories — Is Judah All Israel? — Leaving Elementary Things Behind — From Orphans To Heirs — The Olive Tree of Israel — One Law, One People — The Two Witnesses And Their Fullness — Called to Be Watchmen — Return, O Virgin Israel! — Y'shua: Epitome of All That Is Israel — An Israel Yet To Come. This Enlarged Edition includes, Maps and Charts — Israel In Progress — Index — Bibliography — Informative Addendum about current Jewish genetic research.

ISBN 1-886987-03-3, Paper, 304 pages $14.95.

Also Available in Spanish!

¿Quien es Israel?

Por Batya Wootten
Traducido al Español por Natalie Pavlik
ISBN 1-886987-08-4, Paper, 320 pages, $14.95, plus shipping.

Who Is Israel?

Now Available as A Study Guide

Who Is Israel? and its companion *Study Guide* are causing a phenomenal stir among Bible Believers! The truth about "both the houses of Israel" (Isaiah 8:14) is causing a reformation in the Body of Messiah! Read the book, study the Guide, and find out why so many are being inspired in this last day.

This Guide can be used as a twelve or twenty-four week Study Course. (Completion Certificates available with quantity orders). The Study Plan is simple: Gather a group of people who will agree to meet for a specified time, one that has an end in sight and a specific goal in mind, such as understanding Israel and their part in Israel. Read and discuss the listed Scriptures with your family and friends. Propose a prior reading of the corresponding chapter(s) in *Who Is Israel?* during the week. Sample Questions are listed in the Study Guide, with Answers in the back. We suggest each person read a section in the Lesson (mostly Scriptures), rotating around the room until completed. Then ask the questions. Reading and discussing the selected texts among brethren builds up peoples faith and makes Scripture come alive with new meaning. This plan calls for minimal preparation on the part of the leader.

If you want fellowship with Believers of like mind, order a case of these Study Guides and get started today!

ISBN 1-886987-08-4, Paper, 288 pages, $12.95, plus shipping. Case of Ten: $85.00, plus shipping.

Ephraim and Judah Israel Revealed

by Batya Wootten
Forward by Angus Wootten

Ephraim and Judah Israel Revealed offers a succinct and updated overview of the material presented in the best-selling seminal classic, *Who Is Israel?*, by Batya Wootten. It includes maps, charts and lists that clarify misconceptions about Israel's Twelve Tribes. Like Batya's other solution driven writings, this book is sure to cause a phenomenal stir among Believers. The truth about both houses of Israel is encouraging a reformation in the Body of Messiah. Read this Scripture-based book and find out what is inspiring Believers everywhere!

Who is Israel? Why do you even need to know?
Because knowing who you are and where you are going is vital to your relationship with the GOD of Israel.
You need to read this book because it will:
> Inspire and encourage you, even change your life
> Help you discover your own Hebraic Heritage
> Put your feet on the road to Zion
Read this Scriptural account of Israel and understand:
> Israel, the Church—the Bible
> The mystery of the "fullness of the Gentiles"
> The "blindness of 'Israel'"
> The Father's master plan for Israel
This guidebook will explain why you:
> Feel something is "missing" in your life
> Have an unexplainable love for Israel and Jewish people
> Feel an urge to celebrate the feasts of Israel

This handbook will help you to:
> Move from religion to relationship
> Unmuddle the muddled doctrines of Christianity
> Properly intercede for "all Israel"
> Remove the stones from Israel's road home
> Live the Shema—the heart of New Covenant faith
> Fulfill the latter-day desires of the Father's heart

The Biblical truths unveiled in this volume will help:
> Put an end to "Christian" anti-Semitism
> Heal divisions in the Body of Messiah
> Cure the plague of "Believer's Boredom"
> Relieve "rootlessness" in non-Jews who love "Israel"

This book:
> Leads us back to our First Love
> Lifts up Messiah Y'shua (Jesus)
> Gives Him His proper place
> Shows how He is the epitome of all that is "Israel"

The revelations that unfold on these pages will enrich your relationship with the Holy One of Israel; it will encourage Jewish and non—Jewish Believers (Judah and Ephraim) to become the fullness of the promised "one new man." Read them and be blessed.

This newest book is an excellent tool that will help those of Messianic Israel accomplish the vital mission of identifying Israelites and helping to restore the Kingdom to the whole House of Israel.

By keeping the book succinct, and hence less expensive, it is attractive to buy it in quantities and to distribute as you would tracts. This little book offers the rewarding opportunity of handing someone a quick read that gives the essence of Messianic Israel teachings.

ISBN 1-886987-11-4 Paper, 80 pages, $ 3.95.

For Quantity Discounts contact:

Messianic Israel Ministries
PO Box 700217, Saint Cloud, FL 34770
1 800 829-8777, or visit the Marketplace at

Israel's Feasts
And Their Fullness
by Batya Wootten

Israel's Feasts And Their Fullness

by
Batya Wootten

As Believers in the Messiah, how do we celebrate the feasts? Do we simply follow the traditions of our Jewish brothers, or is there something more we need to see about Israel's appointed feasts? To answer, we need to ask ourselves *why* we celebrate. Once we understand *why* so many non-Jewish Believers now feel called to honor the feasts, our answer will show us *how* to celebrate. The answer to "why" will inspire us as to "how." Understanding why we celebrate will also encourage us and help us to recognize why we feel as we do, and will add a rewarding sense of purpose to our celebrations. This inspiring book addresses the feasts for the people of Messianic Israel and offers suggestions for celebration, whether you are alone or with great numbers. It presents everything in light of our faith in Messiah Y'shua and in light of the role we are to play in bringing restoration to all Israel. Chapters Include: Who Is Celebrating and Why — The Return of The Prodigal, The Purpose of Celebration — Shabbat, Burden or Blessing — Havdallah, The First New Covenant Meeting? — New Moons — Celebrating The Four Passovers — Unleavened Bread — The First of First Fruits and the Resurrection — Shavuot and Two Unleavened Loaves — Yom Teruah and The Twin Silver Trumpets — Yom Kippur and You — Tabernacles and Y'shua — Tabernacles and The Great Day. Also includes Celebration Instruction pages for Shabbat, Havdallah and Passover. (Available Spring, 2002.)

ISBN 1-886987-02-5, Paper 384 pages, $16.95,

EPHRAIM IN DEED

The Lost Tribes and Their Fulfillment of Prophecy *by John Hulley* Does the Bible foretell what the Ephraimites should be doing today? If so, to identify them, we have only to look for the people who are fulfilling those prophecies. Decades of research by Harvard-educated John Hulley have resulted in a convincing account of Ephraimite activities from the Assyrian exile down to our time. Shows their role in the continuing battle for the restoration of Israel and reveals what they will be doing next. (Summer '02).ISBN 1-886987-10-6, Paper, 320 Pages, $16.95.

Ephraim Who? *by Jill Chamberlain Hulley.* This 10- week Bible study has helped many Believers find a biblical basis for what they have sensed to be true: they are part of Ephraim. Ideal for group or individual study, the book takes you from the tribes beginning in Genesis to their glorious end in Revelation. Reinforcing the biblical truth are findings from John Hulley's research into the tribes' itinerary and subsequent history. Compelling evidence of how they are fulfilling their prophetic destiny. ISBN 1-886987-13-0, 36 Pages, Spiral bound, 8 1/2x 11, $8.00.

Ephraim In Sixty Minutes *by Jill Chamberlain Hulley* Ever wondered where the lost tribes went, who they are? Or, what's the point of finding them? This booklet provides answers. Ideal for those new to the subject, it is an appetizer for *Ephraim Who?* An in depth Bible study into the two House truth, this book features some of the findings from John Hulley's forthcoming book—which shows how the tribes are fulfilling their prophetic destiny in history and across continents. ISBN 1-886987-12-2, 96 Pages, Spiral bound, 8 1/2x 11,$15.00.

My Beloved's Israel
by Gloria Cavallaro

Deepen your personal relationship with your Bridegroom. Embark on an intimate journey into the heart of our Heavenly Father. Experience relationship with the Holy One of Israel like David describes in his Psalms. Know intimacy with the Bridegroom like Solomon speaks of in his Song of Songs. Gloria, a spirit-filled Believer, chronicles her visions and dreams, then interprets/journals them in light of Scriptural reflection. Israel must be reunited if they are to be prepared for coming latter-day challenges. This journal exhorts, encourages intimacy with the Holy One and helps prepare ones heart. ISBN 1-886987-05-X 384 pages, $16.95

ALL ISRAEL DANCES TOWARD THE TABERNACLE
by Chester Anderson and Tina Clemens

This inspiring book will help you understand the dynamics of worship. It takes you beyond the pale of other worship books and answers your many dance related questions. For example, What is dance? — How did it originate? — What if I don't know how to dance? — Does something special happen in the Heavenlies when we dance? — What attitude should be in our hearts when we are dancing and why? — Why do I feel so drawn to Hebraic dance? — Why has Davidic dance become so popular? — How does dance come into play in the restoration of both the houses of Israel? This book will fill your heart with hope for the Glory that is soon to be upon us! It will set your feet a dancin'.

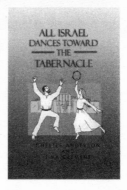

ISBN 1-886987-09-2, Paper, 192 pages. $12.95.

Journey Through Torah Volume I: Commentary on the Torah, Haftarah and Brit Chadoshah Portions for Messianic Israel

by Rav Mordechai Silver

Rav Silver offers Fifty-Two encouraging Torah teachings especially for Messianic Israel —all based on the Jewish tradition of reading certain "portions" of the Torah and the Prophets each week. Comments are founded on the truth that Yahweh is presently reuniting the two sticks of Judah and Ephraim. Silver, a Jewish Believer in the Messiah, repeatedly reaffirms that reunion. Corroborating teachings from the Brit Chadoshah (New Covenant) are included, plus a calendar/listing which lists each of the portions. Inspiring regular readings for those seeking to return to their Hebraic roots. Those who long for Israel's full restoration won't want to miss these enlightening teachings.

ISBN 1-886987-10-6, Paper, 288 pages $14.95, plus shipping.

Want More Torah Teachings?

Want more teachings from both the Old and New Covenants?

Register at our web site and you will receive weekly email Torah Commentaries and teachings from Rav Silver, and other Messianic Israel leaders and teachers.

Go to Registrations at <messianicisrael.com>.

Our Torah Commentaries are posted in the Torah for Today section of our web site. Go to Torah for Today, then to Messianic Israel's Torah Commentaries, at <messianicisrael.com>.